Helping Children Grieve
Ruth P. Arent, M.A., M.S.W.

A GRIEFSTEPS GUIDE

WWW.GRIEFSTEPS.COM

CHAMPION PRESS, LTD.
FREDONIA, WISCONSIN

ISBN: 1891400746
LCCN: 2004110037
Manufactured in the United States of America 10 9 8 7 6 5 4 3 2 1

Author's Note

I feel privileged to contribute to the Grief Steps series. I admire these excellent books and hope that *Helping Children Grieve* will be a worthy addition.

Unlike many books on grieving, this book presents a plan that can effectively promote and enhance parent–child communication during the grieving process. Parents who are anxious for the children to recover from a death will welcome the signs of healing described in *Helping Children Grieve*. Most important, the book contains specific recommendations and upbeat suggestions for parents to help their children recover, and is presented in a spirit of optimism.

Helping Children Grieve covers the topics of multiple trauma, terrorism, and grief by proxy—a much needed supplement. These problems are more likely to confront children today than in the past and parents who are helping children recover will benefit from an understanding of how significant losses affect children.

I can't ask you to "enjoy" this book, because it is always with a lump in the throat that one delves into the world of suffering children, but I hope you will find it worthwhile.

Thank you for all you do for your children in stressful times. . . and in happy times as well.

CONTENTS

Introduction

Wouldn't it be wonderful if we could protect children from ever having to suffer a loss or having to enter into the world of fear and insecurity? Wouldn't it be great if we could keep them safe from injuries and despair? Unhappily, there are no magic wands to wave away sad events, devastating accidents and illnesses, and cruel losses. But loving parents, as caretakers, are destined to be healers so that their children may recover and become fulfilled and successful. This is a masterful task, and it abounds in pain and empathy. It requires endless patience and the everlasting hope that each child will have the strengths and wellness to regain spontaneity and maintain a love of life.

Helping children grieve is a heartrending responsibility. May the insights, information and suggestions offered in this book serve as your special staff as you and your children progress through healing together.

CHAPTER ONE

Back to Basics

"No one paid any attention to me! It was as if I wasn't even there! Didn't anybody remember that he was my daddy and I will never see him again?" Buddy asked forlornly.

Buddy's father died 25 years ago—before many grownups became aware that children grieve, that they grieve in their own way, and that they need a lot of love, support, and understanding when the death occurs and for a long time afterwards.

Young children may appear to be less profoundly moved by a death than adults, but the appearance is deceiving. Children's displays of grief may be long-lasting or very brief. Little children may be distracted fairly easily, perhaps reflecting their belief that death is reversible, while older children may appear to be unaffected, acting bravely so as not to upset others.

Children do not grieve in the same way as adults. The four stages of grief—categorized by Elizabeth Kubler-Ross—are shock and disbelief, searching and yearning, disorganization and despair, and rebuilding and healing. Adults progress through these stages, but children processing grief do not necessarily go through the phases in a predictable way. Rather, in the course of their grief, the phases will appear in random order or in bits and pieces, or they may go back and forth.

Children should be told about a death immediately. They are entitled to the facts. Usually the news should come from a family member, preferably a parent. (When a child's parent has died, it is best that the news come from the surviving parent.) Adults should avoid such phrases as, "We have lost grandpa," "Jamie has gone to live with God," or "Mom is just asleep." One child who was told Grandma was "lost," responded, "Well, let's go find her!"

Children older than five should be allowed or encouraged to attend the funeral, memorial, or celebration of life. The service may be a meaningful closure as well as a chance for the child to understand how much the deceased was loved and admired by others. Rehearsing what will happen at the service may help the child know what will be seen and heard. Should there be organ or body donation or cremation, these procedures need to be explained to the child. "In cremation, the body is turned into soft ashes by a very hot fire. These special ashes are put into a container called an urn." For donation, the explanation may be, "Mom gave permission to give part of her body to an ill person. She gave life to someone else."

Children need to be helped to understand that dying does not mean rejection. A child may wail, "I wet my pants and my daddy got mad! He really didn't love me and now he's gone." She sees the death as punishment and rejection.

Telling your child the truth can prevent unnecessary self-blame and feelings of rejection. "Daddy had a heart attack. His heart stopped beating and he couldn't breathe any more! It had nothing to do with you!" In the case of suicide, the explanation is simply that the deceased person had serious problems and decided to solve them by ending his or her life.

When a parent dies, the child's loss is different from that of the surviving parent. The child has lost a nurturer, protector, teacher, and role model. The adult has lost a partner, friend, lover, and companion. Each will have different needs.

Children are appropriately self-concerned. *What will happen to me?* and *Who will take care of me now?* are predictable questions. Give reassurances that important changes will not occur immediately if such is the case. Tell the children they will not have to move out of their home, change schools, give away pets, go live with a relative or friend, or be placed in a home with strangers even for a very short time. If you must make a major change, try to take the children's feelings into account as much as possible. If, for example, you must move, let the children select the toys and books they want; arrange the moving dates so that the soccer season will be over, or your son or daughter can take part in a graduation ceremony. Keep in mind that major changes will be difficult for all.

Youngsters also need reassurance that they will not have to fill the shoes of the deceased. A child cannot carry the burden of a parent's grief. These bereaved children are still children and they are entitled to be with their friends, continue activities at school and elsewhere, and be encouraged to have experiences that are comforting or distracting, such as going to a movie or playing in a soccer game.

Children may nag adults to repeat again and again every detail of what occurred. They make this demand primarily not to get attention, but as a way to absorb and adjust to their loss one piece at a time. Adjusting to the loss is particularly difficult if, for example, the child was injured in a fatal accident and has to endure his or her own physical and emotional recovery complicated by feelings of survivor guilt.

Caring Ways for a Caregiver To Provide Help
Whether you see a child briefly or you and the child are together a lot, it is best to...

❖ Be available to be a listener—for brief moments or long conversations.

❖ Be honest. EXPRESS YOUR FEELINGS.

❖ Avoid any criticisms or impatience, much less belittling questions, such as "Don't you think you've cried enough today?"

❖ Provide a place for the child to be alone if that is what he or she wants. Allow the child to be uninterested in what is happening. Sometimes children have to regroup, just like adults.

❖ Provide play materials, paints, clay, sand, mud, or soapsuds for the younger children, who may act out their feelings. If young children build a casket out of blocks and climb in and out, do not be upset or alarmed. Such activities are a way for children to discover the realities they seek. Journals for older boys and girls can serve the same purpose.

❖ Arrange for the children to have a reprieve from emotional "gloom and doom" by going to the movies, or visiting relatives or friends. (However, do not send a recently bereaved child to camp for an extended stay.)

❖ Hug, hold, and hug some more. Even teenagers may welcome a hug or a backrub. Young children may want to sleep in the same room with a parent or older sibling for a time.

CHAPTER TWO

Special Considerations for Children by Age

The Baby: Birth to Two Years

Reactions: Yes, a baby will react to the loss of a parent or caretaker. The absence will be sensed and the change in the emotional atmosphere will upset the baby. A baby's responses may include changes in crying and eating patterns, irritability, withdrawal, and a marked increase in thumb-sucking and crying. Both infants and toddlers will sleep in the fetal position. In toddlers, clinging and an onset of temper that may not have been noticed before are common reactions. The "terrible twos" may be more difficult to manage or comfort.

Recommendations: Hold the child often. Follow established routines as best you can, because it will provide some feelings of security. Play with the child and read books. If the child is verbal, as some two-year-olds are, answer questions in a vocabulary the child will understand. It is okay to say, "Mommy is dead. She will not be able to come and take care of you ever again. But I am here to love you and take care of you." To say something like, "But she still loves you," may be very confusing.

Children Ages Two to Six

Reactions: A child this age does not understand that death is permanent. For some children, this understanding may be unusually difficult, because of the coming and going of characters on TV who are mortally ill or injured one day, and running around the next. It's very confusing. Children need help to become accustomed to the words "died" and "dead." A younger child may ask, "Who deaded Mom?" "Can she still eat?" or "Do doggies die too?"

There may be signs of physical distress. Eating habits may change (the child may eat too much or too little), and the child may experience bowel or bladder problems, stomachaches, headaches, or rashes. The child may regress and revert to previously mastered behaviors, such as thumb-sucking, bed-wetting, being unable to tie shoes, having temper tantrums, or clinging to a blankie, a favorite toy, or you. The child may be unusually demanding. Look for the normal fears of this age to intensify, such as fear of the dark, of going to bed, of going to a new place, of a family member leaving and being left with a stranger, and of being taken to a new place, such as a daycare center or preschool.

Emotional swings can be expected—periods of anger, sadness, and anxiety—along with outbursts and withdrawal. These emotions may be accompanied by pleas for the return of the dead person and even direct expressions of guilt. "I screamed at my mom before I went to school and maybe that is why she had the accident." Reassurances are imperative.

Recommendations: These little guys and dolls are incredibly astute observers of the people around them. Therefore, caregivers must share feelings of grief and sadness, thereby modeling a natural response to death.

A preschooler thinks big people are omnipotent. If you use euphemisms such as "Ken has gone away," the child will reason that big people can bring him back if they want to. Similarly, their concept of time is limited. Children may ask frequently when the dead person is coming back, and only with more maturity will be able to understand that the dead person cannot come back because he or she died. The only thing you can do is to tell the truth, over and over again. "Mommy cannot come back." "Daddy loved you, but he died and is not coming home." When you are talking to little ones, it is best to bend down to make eye contact. Never laugh at their questions or consider them cute or silly.

As understanding expands, so too does a child's bank of worries. "If old people die and my dad is old, will he die too?" "If Mommy has a headache, does that mean she is going to die?" These thoughts are usually fleeting; few children dwell on them day after day. If a child does dwell on them, again, tell the truth over and over and offer repeated reassurances. "Daddy is not so very old," or "Most headaches don't mean anything is wrong."

If taking a child to day care is necessary, the parent or caretaker should stay with the child the first few days until the child can anticipate some of the routines and feels confident that the caretaker will come for him or her, as other parents pick up their boys and girls every day.

Children Ages Seven or Eight to Ten

Reactions: Children this age may exhibit on-again, off-again reactions to loss. They alternately approach and then avoid their feelings. A child may withdraw and refuse to interact with anyone, retreating to a bedroom or into a closet. The times a child withdraws are private times to cry or wail or experience numbness, and withdrawal is a meaningful way for children of this age to process their grief. If other family members make frequent references to the death, some children will protest, which is an indicator that the child is coping with the loss and apparently doesn't have a great need to ask many questions.

They become accepting of the reality of death, which may cause some fearfulness and concern for their own mortality. Perhaps the most vivid grief response is anger toward the world and anyone who gets in the way, especially the surviving parent.

Going back to school for bereaved children has its benefits and problems. Schoolwork may suffer if the child is unable to concentrate or is preoccupied with the loss. In her lovely book, *How It Feels When a Parent Dies,* Jill Krementz quotes children as saying that they were afraid they would be pitied and that they noticed other kids didn't know what to say. Some worried that they would be ostracized. On the other hand, the routine gives the children some stability and the warmth of friends is welcome.

Recommendations: In general, you may want to help your child verbalize questions, some of which may be very personal. On the infrequent occasions that children of this age do open up, their questions may be seeking gory details in the case of an accident or violence. It is helpful to start talking about these questions at home and with your child's chosen friends before the child returns to school.

When a child withdraws, reassure the child that you know where he or she is, and that you appreciate the need to be alone. Tell the child that you will check back every few minutes only to express your concern. Do not cajole a child to be sociable and interact with others. These privacy retreats may occur intermittently for periods of up to several hours, especially during the first few days. They will normally become less frequent and of shorter duration. It is essential that you be respectful if you mention the child's withdrawal to visitors or other family members.

Make sure that your child goes to school regularly as soon as possible. Not only is it important to re-establish routine, school is in a sense an escape from the solemnity at home. You may talk to your child's teachers about easing up on academic expectations for a while, and you yourself may want to lower your expectations temporarily. You may also become a little more involved in helping with homework for a time.

Children's grief work may be helped by their teachers and classmates, who make up a child's "second family." The classroom can be a safe place to express grief. If your child is worried about being pitied, explain that for some youngsters, pity is the only way they know to express sympathy, and in doing so they are well intentioned. In truth, everyone may benefit as each little person is learning the life-long lessons of sympathy, compassion and patience.

The Preadolescent and Adolescent

Reactions: The reactions of a teenager to a death in the family depend on his or her maturity, relationship with the deceased, role in the family, understanding of the needs of others, and much more. In general, by emulating adults, a teenager shows maturity in a crisis, reaches out to others, and puts personal needs aside. He or she may feel intense pain, but appears strong and controlled except around peers. Support from peers may be openly given and greatly appreciated, and the tears of friends seem to validate their grief.

As time goes on, in comforting younger siblings, preteen boys and girls seem to be the most sensitive to the needs and feelings of the little ones, whereas the teenagers may seek to escape from the scene, looking for time with their friends, which is completely understandable.

Because teenagers experience stress on many levels under normal circumstances, having to handle a death may put kids of this age on overload. Some disturbing symptoms may be persistent depression, loss of interest in school and activities, a retreat from friends and family, use of drugs or alcohol, unmitigated anger and physical problems like weight loss or gain, sleeplessness and psychosomatic complaints. Some sexual acting out may also take place.

Recommendations: What do these older youngsters need? Very much the same array of adult support as the younger children. Perhaps at the top of the list would be time to be with their friends. Next, someone who will listen, someone who makes them feel important and respected. They also need encouragement to stay in school and do well, and advice to refrain from inappropriate behaviors, such as joining a gang. Provide them with a way to express emotions, such as creative classes, athletics, music, or acting, and give them the time to enjoy reading for entertainment as well as to broaden knowledge.

It is recommended that older children be consulted when arrangements for the funeral or other service are being planned. This consultation indicates respect and awareness, which are so often neglected when there is a tragedy in the family. Beyond this planning, however, a teenager should be discouraged from trying to adopt the role of a missing parent, although there may be more tasks and chores to do.

☀

Final Thoughts

It is important to praise a child of any age when he or she shows patience and compassion towards a grieving person. This act of unselfishness is a noteworthy indicator that someone is coping with his or her own pain while maintaining a sense of balance and community with others.

There is no timeline for recovery. That is one of the fundamental truths in dealing with grief and grieving people. Children's recovery can be so spotty and outward appearances may cover their struggles to accept the void that will be there forever. It is a struggle indeed.

CHAPTER THREE

Scheduled Parent–Child Sharing Times

Understandably, in the chaos that often follows a death, a parent may not be able to find the time to talk to a child alone. The parent may be too upset as well.

It is recommended that the parent establish scheduled parent–child sharing time as soon as possible. Sharing times are simply designated times—appointments if you prefer—when the parent will meet alone with the child in order to give full attention and support. The appointment signals concern for the child and his or her paramount need to be heard—and for many—to be held. Sharing times are especially necessary for children over the age of two.

Sharing builds respect, perhaps an aspect of the parent–child relationship in need of being bolstered or reestablished when a death has occurred. A death in the family can upset even the steadiest of relationships because, when emotions are freely expressed, there can be inadvertent misunderstandings or even conflict. Feelings of neglect and abandonment are all too common. Besides building respect, sharing times are a unique opportunity for children to get to know a parent better and to feel closer and more secure.

How to Introduce Scheduled Parent–Child Sharing Times

Using an "I" message, extend an offer: "I want to help you in as many ways as I can. I know that it is important that we have time together. I am going to set aside time for us to be together and for each of us to share. I want to know how you are feeling and what's going on." With school-age children, times can be worked out together. Be sure to write the appointments on the calendar!

Sharing times are a one-to-one arrangement. Make certain that each child knows that the time will be private. It is not for the family and for sharing with siblings. Siblings are known to hide feelings and concerns from each other, and with all the new adjustments that are going on, "public disclosure" would be unwelcome and unproductive. The scheduled parent–child sharing should always be safeguarded by privacy and be interruption-free.

A Plan for
Scheduled Parent–Child Sharing Times

Age:	2 to 4 years
Approximate Time:	10 minutes (not at bedtime)
Frequency:	Daily
Suggested Content:	Acknowledge your child's feelings of loss, sadness and confusion.
	Introduce the concept of the finality of death.
	Answer all questions.
	Share yourself: "I miss Mommy, too."
	Give reassurances about safety: "I will take care of you." "You are loved." "You will not be left alone."
Signs of Healing:	Seems less fearful and is more at ease with any new adults in his or her life, such as a new babysitter.
	Separation anxiety less intense.
	Need to hold on to deceased person's clothes or picture, or for rituals starts to diminish.
	Improvement in sleeping.
	Decrease in crying.
	Less clingy.
	Regressive behaviors disappear.
Age:	4 to 7 years
Approximate Time:	10 minutes
Frequency:	2 or 3 times per week
Suggested Content:	Make certain your child understands that your scheduled time together is important to you.
	Let your child introduce what he or she wants to talk about. Answer all questions.
	Share your feelings: "I miss Dad a lot." "I feel upset when there are so many decisions to make."
	Give reassurances: "You will feel better soon." "It will become easier to have fun." "Sad mo-

	ments will come and go."
Signs of Healing:	Fewer body complaints.
	Begins to make more decisions and choices—what to wear, what to eat, whom to play with, selecting books for adults to read, selecting toys to play with, and where to sleep.
	More accepting of loss.
	More cheerful, more spontaneous laughter, and increased friendliness.
	Questions about loss are age-appropriate: Where is Heaven? Can Daddy see me?
Age:	8 years to preteen
Approximate Time:	15 minutes
Frequency:	2 or 3 times per week
Suggested Content:	Talk about communication: "Are you having an easier time talking with your friends about Mom?" "Is it easier for your friends to talk about it to you?" "
	Urge your child to share feelings.
	Talk about school, activities and lessons. Is the child overloaded considering that grief can be both distracting and debilitating? Are changes in order?
	Offer a journal.
	Consider talking about self-pity. Preteen girls may be prone to considerable self-pity and need help to ease off.
Signs of Healing:	Retelling what happened becomes less compulsive.
	Anxiety starts to diminish.
	Less spacey, distracted, and agitated.
	Nervous habits become less pronounced.
	Concentrating more at school.
Age:	Teenagers

Suggested Time:	20 minutes
Frequency:	2 or 3 times a week (Tell them that the time limit is made out of respect for their other responsibilities or desires——homework, time with friends, TV, activities, sports, etc.)
Suggested Content:	Express appreciation for all they have done for others in the family. Talk about trust. Confront feelings of self-blame and guilt. Reaffirm boundaries and responsibilities. Specifically explain that the teenager is not responsible for the surviving parent's well-being. Talk about how home tasks may increase, including more time helping younger children. Reassure the teenager that you understand that talking to friends may be easier than your scheduled sharing times, but it is still important to you because you want to know where encouragement or help might be beneficial. Discuss depression, mourning, and grief in as many aspects as possible. Discuss suicidal thoughts. Explain what professional help offers. Reaffirm that it is safe to build new relationships and welcome happiness. Be clear that no substance abuse or addictive behavior is acceptable, including repetitive risk-taking. If they have an interest, talk about cosmic, metaphysical, and spiritual concerns, including life after death, reincarnation and transmigration of the soul. The interests can be intense and should be respected. These concerns indicate personal growth that may promote healing. Urge teenagers not to pull away to the extent that parent–child sharing is abandoned. Continue to encourage creativity—journaling, painting, dancing, reading, theater, and travel. Encourage them to get plenty of rest and exercise.

Signs of Healing:	Increasingly expresses optimism and hope.
	Appears to have accepted the loss and signs of self-pity diminish.
	Makes references to death less frequently.
	Grieves in private.
	Reminisces without intense emotions.
	Possibly shows increased interest in spiritual aspects of death, immortality, and afterlife.
	Shows enthusiastic participation in school and preparing for life after high school or college.
	Reaches out to others.
	May enjoy a close relationship with a role model of the same sex as the deceased parent.

The program for each age group lasts approximately four months. The four-month period should include at least one holiday, when closeness among grieving family members is crucial for healing. There may be spontaneous follow-up sharing times in which you can talk about any feelings and concerns that your child may have.

Encouragements

"Healing takes place if you are willing." This thought affirms that adults can make the rational choice to grieve and heal. NOT SO WITH CHILDREN. They want to feel better now. It hurts. They want someone to make it go away.

When a child is struggling with a death (or other trauma), encouragement can do wonders. It is like holding the hand of toddlers who are learning to walk. At first, they hold your hand tightly, then progress to holding a single finger, and at last, they let go.

You can encourage your child to let go. That is, your child can accept what has happened and move ahead, inspired by your encouragement and his or her determination and spirit.

Here are some encouraging things to say to your child. They are in no particular order and some will pertain to your child, while others may not. Choose the ones that are right for you and add some of your own.

❖ Everyone wants to feel better as soon as possible, but healing takes time.

❖ Don't be afraid to cry. Tears are healing.

❖ Find time to do something for somebody else if you can. Read to your little brother, help your big sister with the dishes, or call your grandparents.

❖ Be a good friend to your friends.

❖ Be patient with yourself and members of your family.

❖ You can handle this situation. Look at what you've already done (for example, greeted visitors with delight).

❖ Let's find a way to keep track of the times when you are NOT feeling sad.

❖ Let's think of something you really want to do and do it! (Watch a favorite TV show, go to the park).

❖ Enjoy school. There are delightful and interesting people there.

❖ Keep pictures where you can enjoy them and remember happy times.

❖ Find someone you trust to tell about something you have done that has pleased you.

Does Your Child Need Professional Help?

Should you become aware that there is a scarcity of signs of healing in your child, you may want to consider getting him or her professional help. Answering these questions will help guide you in your decision.

Is your child. . .

❖ Depressed, immobilized, or feeling hopeless?

❖ Showing emotional swings that are greatly exaggerated, with extended periods of anger or fear?

❖ Acting out with anger and hostility—even cruelty—to others or animals?

❖ Continuing to yearn for the dead loved one, to the detriment of schoolwork?

❖ Showing new symptoms of trauma, or showing recurring manifestations of old symptoms after they had subsided?

❖ Refusing support from family or others?

❖ Abounding in physical complaints, weight problems, sleeping problems, nightmares, or nervous habits?

❖ Prone to suicidal thoughts?

❖ Threatening to quit school or run away?

❖ Defiant, obstructive, or creating nonstop stress and problems in the family?

Keep in mind that a professional may recommend medication, which would be ordered and supervised by a mental health physician.

Be proud of your decision to get help for your child. The trauma occurred; your child has endured an assortment of emotions and being a young person, has not been able to sort them out and learn to cope as you had hoped he or she would. You are exercising your compassion and wisdom when you arrange for your child to work with someone who has the skills to give a child support, clarity, and direction. Don't feel badly or embarrassed that you couldn't meet all of your bereaved child's needs, because some can be met only by a professional. In the future your children may well come to you and thank you for sending them to see a "shrink" or a social worker.

One final thought: Avail yourself of counseling as well if you feel overwhelmed, dysfunctional, or just plain depressed. Remember, you are entitled to a boost too!

CHAPTER FOUR

Life Isn't Always Fair: Multiple Layered Traumas

The child in the corner is trembling. Not a tear, not a wail, but she looks so tragically forlorn that it is heartbreaking. What has this little person had to endure that accounts for such despair? Her expression portrays hopelessness. How can she be helped to feel better?

It is a myth that if a person has had to face one trauma after another, he or she will become stronger, more stalwart, and less despairing. That is not true. The ability to withstand trauma and recover diminishes with each event, and the person who has suffered multiple traumas needs more help to recover and regain the fortitude to face the future with whatever it may hold. Children may have never developed the coping skills needed to recover on their own; they need *considerable* help through their grieving.

If more than one person is killed in an accident, the event is a multiple trauma for the survivors. So too is the death of a parent, sibling, or friend following the trauma of a divorce, disruption due to a calamity, personal failures, or major disappointments of many kinds. The length of time between the traumas is incidental in that the memory unfortunately brings forth old responses that are weighted with the after affects of sadness, confusion, bewilderment, anger, and all the other emotions associated with the event gone by.

My "instructions" to you as a parent are to not pretend you don't know what you know. If your child or the child you are consoling has suffered multiple traumas, *you know it*. You know about a death, a divorce, a home fire, an accident, or whatever the child suffered. You know that the child now feels more overwhelmed and helpless than ever before. *This child needs special considerations from you now.*

Ways to Approach, Console and Comfort a Child

In approaching a child who has experienced multiple-layered traumas, be gentle. The child may feel overwhelmed and suspicious of all adults. Tell the child openly, "I want to comfort you." By your demeanor, let the child know he or she is safe with you. Whether at home, in a hospital, or at a mortuary, you will not invade his or her space. You may smile softly. You may display your concern with nary a word.

Regarding affection, a small child may welcome a snuggle and a shoulder to cry onto. Older children may not. In experiencing shock and numbness, some children are not prepared to be touched. In a few minutes—or perhaps much later—the child may welcome a touch or a pat. Even a mother or father would be wise to ask. Asking for permission to touch a child shows respect and if the child is feeling shattered, this small bit of dignity is meaningful.

If the child moves away from you or does not respond, do not take it personally. Not wanting to be touched is a symptom of profound upset. Be patient. Repeat the request. A laconic "okay" may be the answer. Older children may qualify their response and add, "It's no big deal."

A death represents a loss of trust, and affection may be a hallmark of trust that a child is not prepared to handle at this time.

Acknowledging Another Loss

You may be the first—or only—person who acknowledges that the death is *another* loss for this child. This acknowledgment can be quite a relief to the little person, as it may bring forth an intense outburst of grief and a gratefulness that somebody understands what it means to take another blow again. An outcry for sympathy may be another response, perhaps reflecting incomplete consolation from the other traumas and the gaping hole that needs to be filled. This child is very needy and you have found a meaningful way to start to offer support.

How you progress with this child will depend in part on the particular situation, but there are some essential things to let a child know at this very early stage that can lay the foundation for healing. As you interact with this sad child, the following ideas may be helpful:

❖ Present yourself as a listener.
❖ Don't give any advice.

❖ Offering to sit together in a quiet, private place or getting a drink or something to eat may be appreciated.

Some children may welcome a few reassuring words about other family members and how they are doing. Children rarely ask other members of their family personal questions during times of upheaval. A comment such as, "Dad seems to be holding up really well, even though this is a very sad time for him too," shows your compassion.

When the child starts to share, make certain you don't interrupt. The child's words may be whispered and hesitant or they may be spoken rapidly with the child facing away from you. If possible, reflect on what was shared. "I understand that you never thought it could be so hard to find out that your sister was killed." If the child should ask questions, such as "What will happen at the cemetery?" or "What does cremated mean?", answer factually.

Once the child has opened up, you may want to ask some questions. Try to assess how severely upset your child is. Also, try to determine how much of this distress is due to what is happening at the moment, and how much is coming from horrible memories or feelings from the past, which can be overwhelming. A child may be having harsh flashbacks. You may want to ask about how he or she recovered before, who helped the most, and what the people who helped said or did. Those memories are positive, an important dimension to inject now amidst the stress and sadness. In talking about these memories with your child, you may find information that you can use to help your child begin grieving anew.

The detailed script given here incorporates an assortment of ways to reach out to a bereaved child. The approach is very conservative because that is necessary for multi-layered traumatized children. You must move gingerly; they are very fragile. Despite their fragility, you may manage to achieve what you set out to do—you provided a few moments of safety and you were respectful, caring and supportive. Those achievements cannot be overly applauded, especially if you are in great pain yourself.

Reaching Out to
Older Boys and Girls and Teenagers

The grief reactions of multi-layered traumatized older children may range from hysterical sobbing to the controlled stoicism of a bystander, one who appears numb or emotionally paralyzed. The most common response of children this age is anger. "Why the (blank) did this have to happen to me?"

Teens may be totally uninterested in anything you have to say or offer. Even though you are aware of past traumas, a teenager is not usually receptive to reminders of them. Older children's disclosures, if they do respond to you, will seldom contain a reference to anything that happened in the past. Dealing with the current loss is where he or she is focused. Kids need to get anger out of their system. That anger can effectively muffle the awareness and display of other symptoms of trauma, which as anger lessens, will have to be confronted at some time during the grieving process, just as with any other death.

Accepting that teens want their privacy, take time to repeat that you have support to offer. Simply remind them, "I am here to help. I am here to listen. Let me know what I can do for you." In turning over the responsibility to them to choose whom they want to be with, you are providing a bit of empowerment that may be welcome. If everything else has been out of their control, your suggestion to let them decide about sharing with you is constructive.

Deaths from Domestic Violence

There are four kinds of death: natural, accidental, homicide, and suicide. In almost all deaths of the latter three types, there is a degree of violence which creates an overlay of anger and anxiety to the grief of the survivors. For children, the combination of disturbing emotions may have serious repercussions. Lost is their trust in the world as a safe place to be, and in adults as protectors. To reestablish their sense of security is an important facet of the healing work that lies ahead—work that parents and children must face together.

Deaths from violence are horribly traumatic, and a death in the family from domestic violence is the most traumatic wound of all. All too often, the violent death, (whether the abuse finally results in homicide, or the abused person turns on the abuser), comes after years of conflict and violence, where an adult was out of control. Further adding to the emotional upheaval is the incredible conflict a child feels toward the violent parent. It is a true love-hate situation at best, rife with fear, frustration, and feelings of powerlessness and rage.

After a domestic-violence homicide, the situation is resolved one way or another, so the family's surviving children may have feelings of *relief*—mixed in with sorrow and even more confusion—along with guilt that they could not have prevented the tragedy. There is a tremendous concern for the well-being of all survivors as well.

Because a death from domestic violence is extremely traumatic, the grieving work a parent or adult must do with the child is complicated. In working with these bereaved children, keep in mind . . .

❖ The tumultuous emotions a child feels after a domestic violence death that must be expressed. It will be painful for you to hear how much your child has suffered from fear, guilt, anger, despair, frustration and impatience, as well as experiencing love, sympathy, empathy and compassion.

❖ It is not the child's fault. This message may have to be repeated many times before the child will come to believe it, but it is essential to the child's healing. The perpetrator's tendency to violence is his or her problem only, and not the child's.

❖ Some questions in life simply have no answers. That is difficult to accept when a child is working through grief. When dad batters mom or mom abuses a sibling, all children in the family are victims too. A child may ask, "Why did Dad pick on Mom and Mary, and not me?" Such questions can cause unbounded discomfort. Be honest with a child—you don't know the answers and are struggling with the questions yourself.

❖ Talk to the child about how he or she could not have repaired or fixed the relationship between the abuser and the abused. There is no way that anyone—adult or child—can negotiate the relationship between others, even family members. Many times in abusive households, a child will want to be a peacemaker, but will see his or her efforts fail again and again. Talking to your child about this difficult life lesson will ease feelings of frustration and powerlessness.

Some children, especially older children, may be able to understand the "battering syndrome," in which tensions build and precipitate a violent episode, which is followed by remorse, apologies, and expressions of love. After a period of peace, tensions build and the cycle repeats. Children become quite agitated as they pick up the clues that violence may take place within a short time, which has harmful effects on schoolwork and family communication.

Therapy for
Survivors of a Domestic Homicide

Every child who has had a family member killed in an incident of domestic violence needs therapy. Every individual is unique and it is very rare that I, as a psychologist, make a blanket recommendation, but this is one time that I do: Please, please, get the child the help of a professional.

Children may be resistant to therapy. In many violent households, the abusive situation has been ongoing for quite some time. A child, especially a teenager, may feel that, "I've dealt with this stuff all my life, and I'm hanging in there." They may want to rely on friends rather than family members or rather than an unknown therapist. Nevertheless, they need help to admit that they haven't faced the fear, anger, and other strong feelings that have become so familiar. If a child has worked out ways to cope, it will be scary to let go of defenses that have seemed to serve well.

It is imperative you get through to a resistant child. "I'm worried about you," is a simple, direct way to express your concern. These messages may be persuasive:

❖ "That was a terrible situation and the problems it created are not going to disappear soon."

❖ "I care enough about you to risk your anger at me if I repeat the suggestion to get therapy."

❖ "I have confidence that help is worthwhile."

Suicide

Adults struggle to understand suicide. Children, too, grope for explanations. After a suicide, there are usually feelings of anger and guilt mixed in with feelings of grief—a hard situation for adults and very confusing to children. If children pick up the message that the suicide should be kept a secret or is something to be ashamed of, they may become even more confused. It is easier for many survivors to accept a death as an "accident" rather than a suicide.

In dealing with suicide, parents should be honest with children and give them appropriate facts. Even if parents still have unanswered questions about the suicide, they may make a clear statement to their children such as, "Uncle Phil killed himself because he thought it was the only way to solve his very serious problems."

There is no need at the time of the death to burden **young** children with details or the danger signs of suicide and the reasons people take their own lives. **Older** boys and girls will most probably demand full explanations of the uncle's problems. "Was Uncle Phil an alcoholic?" "Did he lose his job?" "Was his cancer getting worse?" may be the first questions asked. Again, deal with the questions honestly and give children age-appropriate facts.

One of the most painful aspects of suicide is that some completed suicides may in fact have been cries for help; the person did not really intend to kill him- or herself. The person is in trouble emotionally and needs help and does not intend to die, but unfortunately, a rescuer does not arrive on time. A woman takes a few pills, knowing that her husband will find her, but he gets caught in heavy traffic coming home from work and is too late to save her.

Most suicidal people are ambivalent. A part of them wants to die, but a part of them wants to live. It is the positive side of the ambivalence that 911 and hotline operators, and other emergency personnel are trained to pick up. Building on the positive, rescue personnel hope to help the distraught person overcome the crisis and get help. However, suicidologists recognize that some people do intend to die, do not reach out for help, and use a method that is sure to work.

Teenagers, unfortunately, are all too familiar with suicide. It is a far too common tragedy in the United States today, with more than 5,000 deaths a year in the teen population. Also, most high schools present programs to advise students how to identify signs of depression and suicidal intent and what to do about it. A list of signals is given below.

In helping your child recover from the suicide of a friend or a classmate, emphasize that should he or she becomes upset, *to please come and talk it over with you.* Remind your child that suicide is a personal choice and that no one else is responsible for the action that took place. Even though others may have tried to help the upset person, their efforts were to no avail.

Signals of Suicide

Learning about the signals of suicide may be considered a next step for a child (or even an adult) who is mourning for a suicide victim. It is positive for a child to feel empowered by knowing that he or she would know when to seek help for a suicidal person. Yes, a grieving person may ruminate that the deceased gave out indicators that were not recognized or dealt with effectively, which may bring about feelings of guilt. However, many relatives and friends of suicide victims feel it is imperative to learn the warning signs of suicide. Similarly, a depressed person may recognize that he or she is in trouble and seek help.

The person...

❖ Gives away favorite possessions.

❖ Has an obsession about death and talks about suicide.

❖ Shows a decline in performance at work or school and other activities.

❖ Takes reckless actions.

❖ Has a deteriorating physical appearance.

❖ Has a marked change in behavior...for example, becoming gleeful after being depressed.

❖ Purchases the means of suicide (a gun, pills, etc).

❖ Reveals a desire to die.

❖ Exhibits symptoms of depression, including crying, insomnia or sleeping a lot, and loss of appetite.

❖ Has made previous suicide attempts.

One of the most common reasons that young children--those younger than 13--attempt or commit suicide is that they have never recovered from the death of a loved one. Their grief had never healed and no one was aware of the ongoing, deep pain, nor responded to it. The problems are particularly severe after the death of a sibling. The dead person was invariably memorialized and frequently absolved of weaknesses or faults, and past troubles were forgotten. The intense and prolonged parental absorption with the loss results in suicidal children's feelings of neglect, unimportance, and resentment. In addition to their own sorrow, they become convinced that they aren't worth very much, and that their future is bleak and perhaps, hoping for a reunion with the deceased sibling after death, they come to believe that suicide is the best decision to make.

There is a vital message implied in the previous paragraph that calls for special attention. *It is imperative that a parent remains aware of how a child is displaying grief.* The parent should monitor what, if any, improvements are evolving in the bereaved child. The parent should also keep a mental inventory of how much attention he or she is paying to the grieving youngster.

Healing takes time—a minimum of six months—but parents are urged to continue to be straightforward and intermittently ask how the survivor is feeling. Have any special memories come up of late (for instance, at the onset of the football season if a dead brother was a player or had a favorite team)? Are memories being stirred up as a holiday approaches? Bear in mind children have picked up clues in the time following the death. They may have learned that you get too upset if they mention the death, so they refrain from doing so. Also, they may be experiencing scorn from others. "Are you still talking about your brother?" is a piercing putdown and it may seriously curtail expressions of grief that are an integral part of healing.

CHAPTER FIVE

Grief by Proxy and Terrorism

W hen a parent, grandparent, sibling or friend dies, it may be a child's first experience with death. The loss is a trauma, a wound that will heal and leave a scar. Unfortunately, some children have experienced many traumas, deaths, abuse, witnessing violence, accidents, illnesses, and natural disasters of terrifying proportions. Children who have experienced multiple traumas will be more profoundly affected by a death because they are burdened with memories and perhaps unresolved grief and anxiety.

Children can also suffer from grief by proxy, which occurs when a person empathizes with the victims of a tragedy and experiences the same emotional reactions and symptoms of traumatic stress. With acts of terrorist violence occurring around the world, trauma by proxy is almost universal, affecting adults and children as well. If a death should occur in your family when there is a traumatic story dominating the news, such as the Oklahoma City bombing, 9/11, or the Beslan school massacre in Russia, your work with the child is more complicated and intense. Without question, attending to the personal loss takes priority. With regard to terrorism, there are some measures that can be taken, such as. . .

❖ Do not give reassurances that this won't happen again, because there are no such reassurances. Do reassure your children that your devotion and stead-fastness are in no way affected by the public tragedy.

❖ Be assertive and limit the amount of TV that the children watch, and take precautions to avoid too much time reading about such tragedies. It has been noted that some adolescents are more traumatized by written accounts than they are by TV reports because newspapers and magazines give more details and sometimes have many intense pictures.

❖ Keep in mind how you yourself are adjusting when your feelings of loss at the death of a loved one are complicated by an overwhelming tragedy. Seek help from others, for the children, as well as for yourself. Be truthful with the children and tell them that you are feeling overwhelmed by using whatever expression your little ones would understand.

❖ Look for serious signs of depression, which may result from past wounds and the current multi-layered traumas. Some children may need monitored amounts of anti-depressants for a while. Preteen girls seem to be particularly vulnerable with crying spells, snappiness, very short attention spans, comments about the meaningless of life, and other verbal messages of despair. If you, teachers, and friends, cannot find effective ways to cheer up the child for more than a brief moment, it is suggested that she be taken to counseling as soon as possible.

❖ Try to find appropriate groups that may interest and benefit you or your grief-stricken child. Although kids may stick together as friends, it is not unusual that they do not disclose their innermost fears, thoughts and feelings. Rather, they talk about football, school gossip, or a movie. However, in a group setting in the presence of a skillful adult, the feelings surrounding their traumatic pain may be shared, and it is likely that they will receive helpful information and advice. Maybe an informal gathering at your house would be worthwhile to introduce the comfort and benefits of sharing.

CHAPTER SIX

What to Believe:
Sorting Out Spirituality and Faith in the Work of Healing

A s a child therapist for almost thirty years, I was aware that some of the most difficult struggles a bereaved child had to contend with were "Why did Bobby die?", "Why was it my dad who was killed in that car?", or "Why couldn't God have prevented my sister from getting leukemia?"

Some of the children were seeking answers to questions beyond the theology of the family religion. Many had no formal credo and were searching for answers to help them accept the reality of the loss and the realization that everything and everyone will die, including themselves. They had to find a way to understand that they were free to work through their pain and regain a sense of well-being and a love of life.

I found that these quotes from Earl Grollman's *Living When a Loved one Has Died* provided a baseline from which to discuss some spiritual matters:

❖ Death is a journey into the unknown.

❖ Your religion may provide you with a philosophical base for confronting moments of darkness and despair.

❖ Religion does not ignore your natural fear of separation.

❖ Your faith offers you a way to share resources in your encounter with helplessness, guilt, and loneliness.

❖ You may find that no event—even death—separates you from God.

Other statements included, for many, the belief in an afterlife that helps dull the pain of awareness of one's finite nature.

❖ Faith offers a source of strength beyond yourself.

❖ Grief shared is grief diminished.

My task was to work with the children in their endeavors to meld their feelings and the mystery of loss with the step-by-step adjustments and improvements they were making, day-by-day. I was the fulcrum of their emotional seesaw. By staying focused on their behaviors and their responses to others, as well as to their emotions, they were able to integrate their uncertainties about spiritual concerns into their healing.

Children as young as ten brought in their thoughts and questions about immortality, life after death, near-death experiences, metaphysical concerns, and well thought out ideas about God as nature, God as an ever-present source of strength, comfort, wisdom, direction, and the like. Without exception, every child, including the teenagers, had the most difficult time overcoming their anger and their immediate concerns for their safety and future.

About one out of every sixteen children will face the death of a parent during childhood. Should you be faced with comforting your child in this situation and the matter of *why* comes up, be straightforward and brief. Extensive explanations, perhaps embellished with biblical quotes, may discourage a child from coming to you for more information.

Children may ask what seems like a profound question and yet it may only be a fleeting thought. That is the world of young children. They look for quick answers, and then go off to watch TV or play with friends. Teenagers may cut off a conversation if what you tell them doesn't happen to agree with what they are thinking, and they prefer not to get into a lengthy discussion. Don't take it personally. Talking about God and death and loss is not easy for anyone, especially youth.

CHAPTER SEVEN

Resiliency, Strengths and Wellness

Human beings are born with an innate self-righting ability—important good news for parents helping a grieving child. Children are blessed with strengths to help them overcome difficulties, attain happiness, and to enjoy successful relationships and accomplishments. Sometimes children confront difficulties that are gargantuan and some children are more vulnerable than others. Some children are fortunate enough to receive the love and support needed to boost them up and sustain them in times of trouble. And you can provide that love and support!

Resiliency is the ability to bounce back. When young children experience a death in the family, or some other loss or trauma, not only is it a setback to be overcome, but also it may impede the way they develop and mature. The task of any grownup caring for a grieving child is to discover the child's strengths and build on them, while providing a sense of safety, trust, availability, and optimism.

For older children, resiliency is reinforced by the attention and support of school friends and teachers as well as coaches, Scout leaders, and others. Your children may benefit from the empathy and sensitivity of such concerned adults.

Strengths and Wellness

Watch for signs of your children's increased strengths and wellness. Out of the sadness of a death, a child can grow and learn. The more signs of wellness your children exhibit, the more they are healing.

❖ Your child tells you that yesterday he cried a little bit.

❖ He has learned that expressing emotions is acceptable.

❖ Your child repeats a joke for you. He giggles more freely, laughs uproariously, and enjoys a bit of teasing.

❖ He has learned the importance of a sense of humor.

❖ Your child confides that she likes the new sitter a lot.

❖ She has learned to turn to new people and enjoy new relationships, and perhaps strengthened or renewed relationships with grandparents, friends, and siblings.

❖ Your child tells you that the dad of a kid in his class was killed, and adds, "I really feel sorry for him."

❖ He has learned that others have had similar experiences and how to empathize with them.

❖ Your child stops sucking her thumb and joins others in playing outside. She tells you, "I still feel very sad, but I forgot about Mom when I was playing with the other kids."

❖ She has learned that nonstop dwelling on a loss (and perhaps self-pity) can be overcome, if only for a short time at first. (With your encouragement, these breaks will occur more often and last longer.)

❖ Your child reads an ad out loud. "Life isn't always fair," and she says, "You can say that again!"

❖ She has experienced a values clarification. You can build on this insight by adding positive comments: "But we have each other. We're both feeling better and have happy times now."

※

Helping children grieve is a precious responsibility. This is not a light-hearted statement; rather it is a heartfelt reminder that children are fragile. Although they progress from the total dependency of infancy, each one remains vulnerable and in need of special handling. Yes, even with God-given strengths and resiliency, they cannot handle grief on their own.

Your children are blessed to have you and you are blessed to have them, because from your reservoirs of devotion, each of you can provide ingredients so necessary for healing.

"What the caterpillar calls
the end of the world, the
master calls a butterfly."
~ **Richard Bach**

Online Support Classes, Groups and Resources

Take a step toward healing with interactive, online courses led by best-selling author Brook Noel

How do the classes work?

It's easy to get started with a GriefSteps class. Simply enroll in the class of your choice at www.griefsteps.com . Once you enroll, you'll receive a welcome packet that will contain directions for the classes.

Now What? Living After Loss

This class offers a solid foundation for anyone wondering how to go on after loss. You'll learn what to expect physically and emotionally, and how to take your first steps toward healing.

Class length – 3 weeks   Cost $19

Rituals to Honor Your Loved One

Rituals are a wonderful way to keep the memory of your loved one with you. This class will introduce you to different types of rituals and guide you in creating one of your own.

Class length – 4 weeks Cost $29

Basic Strategies and Exercises for Healing

In this interactive, online course, you'll complete 4 different exercises that can help you on your grief journey. You'll also learn what to expect on your journey and strategies for coping.

Class length – 3 weeks Cost $19

Grief Resources from Grief Steps®

I Wasn't Ready to Say Goodbye: Surviving, Coping and Healing After the Sudden Death of a Loved One by Pamela D. Blair, Ph.D. and Brook Noel (14.95) ISBN 1-891400-27-4; Companion Workbook also available (18.95) ISBN 1-891400-50-9

Grief Steps: 10 Steps to Regroup, Rebuild and Renew After Any Life Loss by Brook Noel ($14.95) ISBN 1-891400-35-5; Companion Workbook also available ($18.95) ISBN 1-891400-34-7

Living with Grief: a guide for your first year of grieving by Pamela D. Blair, Ph.D. and Brook Noel, adapted from *I Wasn't Ready to Say Goodbye: Surviving, Coping and Healing After the Sudden Death of a Loved One* ($8.95) ISBN 1-891400-08-8

Surviving Holidays, Birthdays and Anniversaries: A Guide for Grieving During Special Occasions by Brook Noel ($8.95) ISBN 1-891400-03-7

You're Not Alone: Resources to Help You On Your Grief Journey by Brook Noel and Pamela D. Blair, Ph.D. ($9.95) ISBN 1-891400-63-0

Understanding the Emotional and Physical Effects of Grief by Brook Noel ($9.95) ISBN 1-891400-77-0

Finding Peace: Exercises to Help Heal the Pain of Loss by Brook Noel and Pamela D. Blair, Ph.D. ($9.95) ISBN 1-891400-78-9

My World is Upside Down: Making Sense of Life After Confronting Death by Brook Noel and Pamela D. Blair, Ph.D. ($9.95) ISBN 1-891400-24-X

Facing the Ultimate Loss: Coping with the Death of a Child by Robert J. Marx and Susan Wengerhoff Davidson ($14.95 paperback, $23.95 hardcover). ISBN 1-891400-99-1, 1891400-93-2.

Grief Steps.Com

Free online reading room, e-mail message board support,
free support newsletters, and more.

Log on today

www.griefsteps.com